Imagination Verses

JENNIFER MOXLEY was born in 1964 and grew up in San Diego, California. As an adult she has lived in Seattle, San Francisco, Providence and Paris. From 1992–1995 she edited *The Impercipient*, a stapled & photocopied magazine dedicated to publishing the work of her contemporaries. Following this venture she co-edited, with her long-time partner Steve Evans, *The Impercipient Lecture Series*, a monthly poetics pamphlet. She has also served as the poetry editor for *The Baffler* magazine since 1997. In addition to her US, Canadian, and British publications, her poetry has been translated into Norwegian, Czech, Swedish and French. Presently she lives in Orono, Maine where she works as an Assistant Professor at the University of Maine.

Imagination Verses

JENNIFER MOXLEY

S
SALT

PUBLISHED BY SALT PUBLISHING
PO Box 937, Great Wilbraham PDO, Cambridge CB1 5JX United Kingdom
PO Box 202, Applecross, Western Australia 6153

First published by Tender Buttons, New York, USA 1996
Second edition 2003

Printed and bound in the United Kingdom by Lightning Source

Typeset in Swift 9.5 / 13

ISBN 1 876857 94 3 paperback

SP

1 3 5 7 9 8 6 4 2

To my Contemporaries

Contents

Acknowledgments

I am grateful to the editors of the magazines in which some poems in this collection first appeared:

Arras, Brian Kim Stefans
The Baffler, Damon Krukowski
Black Bread, Sianne Ngai & Jessica Lowenthal
Chain, Juliana Spahr & Jena Osman
Dark Ages Clasp the Daisy Root, Ben Friedlander
Exact Change Yearbook #1, Peter Gizzi
Letterbox, Scott Bentley
Lingo, Michael Gizzi
Mirage#4/Period(ical), Kevin Killian & Dodie Bellamy
Object, Rob Fitterman
o.blek, Peter Gizzi & Connell McGrath
Phoebe, Jean Donnelly
13th Moon, Katie Yates
Troubled Surfer, Lisa Jarnot
The World, Lewis Warsh

"The Ballad of Her rePossession" was published as a section of *re:Chapbook #1*, reference: press 1995, edited by Beth Anderson.

"Helena & the Regional Boys" was a Tender Broadside, Tender Buttons 1993.

Preface

OUR STATES, whether social or organic, are composed of effects both chosen (verses) and not (Imagination). When we hope for a future different from the present we uncover the injustice of our imagination. We find the scales of value during the slow climb towards maturity and knowledge, as we journey towards the completion of what Valéry called our "whole training in the *possible*." The "possible" is by its very nature unequal. Though we may dream the dream of equality, we dream it on a scale much larger than ourselves. If we try to make a poem of this dream, it will be smaller than its origins. Being time-based beings, we cannot escape compromise, concealing history with each new life, born to begin the accumulation of knowledge from zero to one and so forth. Poetry is the frustration of such limits. As an art form, it is a bridge of half measures on the way to the possible, drawn from the viewpoint, time frame and landscape of a single life. The poem is unjust in its largesse, an axis point through which the creator and the community of a shared language pass. The poem offers a history of and a future for the mind's prerogative to exist as more than a memory of its milieus. It is a small but necessary intervention, a crucial and critical disjuncture.

For all the violence sprung from the official versus the unofficial book, where literature is found has less to do with its force than who we are when we find it. Are we ready to receive it? Many have come to literature from strange paths and pieced it together to their own liking, ignoring all the established orders. Poetry is not for the passive. It is, as Mayakovsky knew, at its very root tendentious. Even the love poem agitates the beloved to fall in love with the poet.

These *Imagination Verses* were written over a five year period (1990–1995) while I lived in Providence. They were not written as a book nor as a series but randomly in fits and starts, and are comprised of a variety of different free verse forms. They were written out of a desire to engage the universal lyric "I," as well as the poetic line, with all of its specific formal artifice.

J.M.

Imagination Verses

What blame to us if the heart live on.

—HART CRANE

Home World

I will say what the register calls forth,

the range of the heart

a journey in the strap of speech,

unrealized, failing to grapple

with even the first word,

or world where I saw humans

in the shadows of buildings

unable to speak at all.

Their dark needs

had grown a weedy tent

over the earth, laid bare.

They could not see

the river for the bank

yet still kept talking

about the bridge.

I lived there too,

saw innocence

among the old

grown willowy.

My illusion could not deflect the float

or the filth upon it,

and all that foliage

what could it have meant

in the light of adornment?

When I remembered nature

as an evil dream

that interrupted my house

and destroyed my family,

leaving me to covet.

I dreamt my sense could wend the fight away

and carnage was my hollow nourishment.

I could have grown tall,

but I awoke to no words and wonder left.

From a Distance I Can See

You have a lovely and familiar gravity,

and like in the apartment of my youthful reveries

each time I walk into you my city-bound Greyhound

rolls through the rain drenched streets,

a lightscape full of traffic and wondrous people

lies ahead, once you've caught view they shall demand

the tapering of all your beautiful fingers,

they shall tell your eyes to stop shooting such glances

for they are blocking your lips from seeming

red as they are, and what of gentle memory,

it frames your face and returns home devastated

to inform me of such boundaries shifting

that in them, as in you, my dreams shall rest just dreams,

the rain drenched city of adulthood, vanish in advances.

I am Depressed without Your Pencil too

This house is one big search for meaning
or a clean dish, but without my dreamed for
vanity who can expect attention to order
or for that matter eternal beauty. This
house is a small space of rearrangements,
a paint box for important revolutions.
All orphaned overstuffs are welcomed here
as are rickety woods. And on that note
broken things may stay as long as they please,
whether or not they maintain their origins.
This house has given us objects to search for
with the comfort that they do exist,
though perhaps just as mementos
of the places that we've left. You're busy
searching for your special pencil
that was last seen around the kitchen table,
and if people would just quit calling
I too could help you look, last seen I think
about the bed when all our friends were out of town.

Night Train to Domestic Living Arrangements

In my own mind you have put me

beside compunction. Re-worked

this mourning room where looking

smacks of mother may I

though to this day I'll falter

when sleep holds sway.

Throw me over your deep end

with some faith next time,

as if to lend some bother to the vex.

I've always wanted to be grown up

like a bureaucrat, a berth-rider

ordering night caps over the Rockies.

But you keep insisting on day planners,

bodies flat out. Which means,

for example, a random plea.

Do some dishes and get back to me.

I'm waiting at the ripping point

breast in hand, a broken spine

like any sign of care.

Not on My Seashore

You drew me under yards

of bad luck and backward lives,

you bucked up yarns

of past beguilers

who tended to shift away

from scripted misery.

Your islands of personality

give no good guidance

when desire breaks up

beauty's trance to leave me

an Emptery waiting for visitors.

It was not I who was enamored

of the sky's insipid blue,

the tilt of fisted history

roped and kinky with the tide.

You drew me like a family,

some false hope factory

from which to call in the new day!

Cut it out and give me that rope,

I will gladly beat my scared Crusoe

with the possibility of life

and orate at the seashore

of luckless sinking blind

and God-blanched Utopias:

But know my heart is on your hands.

Ode on the End

In afterlife
I stood
and wished the depths
of fright
to crumble
by random
weights and measures.
I could not feel
my morals
at the borders
of darkness, I
was left alone
by an unfinished
thought, like a fool.
I found that lack
of place, un-
imaginable after-
math all on
my own. My discovery
so emptied me
a stairwell
into Hell
would have seemed

most welcoming,

a landscape, death red,

the moderate grade

of enemies

gradually accustomed

to anything

the mind

might think. The mere

recognition of it

would be at least

a seed of sense

to wish a future

up from. And yet

to my eye

from this vacant

drape

a better place

appeared, equal measures

of air and earth

came to me

precious enough,

I wore them

well knowing

my thoughts

would think me

hollow, exiled

to the abandoning

company

of all

my illusory

ends.

Bi-coastal Fleshings

This in-wrought geneticism
has made your leniency all askew,
a melee on the installment plan,
like chance encounters with minikin emotions
unstitch Minerva and the Earth awakes
distracted reaching for Venus.
For years you've been grabbing power so,
knowing lest you crumble there's always class
to catch you in its bibelots—
down that rabbit hole my liege
I'm a camera gathering brightness
my ligature of future imaginings
somehow assured the universe will unravel
light and dark despite the wile of while.

Fin de Siècle Go-betweens

There you are in the hinterland chiseling

Nations into the ocean as I await torrential

winds. In our search for beauty we've left

our footprints for the Native informers of narcissism

to uncover once we've fled. We should have let

the out-of-work jesters jingle gun toters

and just gone on with the Eros of coastal waters.

I'll hide your lesser self inside this bird of paradox,

a place dispatchers won't mistake it for any

errant sign of life. While we've been talking

they've lined up along the border towns

heavy with wistfulness, so if ever lip service

might save the planet let's hope it's now,

jettison that charm however and we might be

the end of something gathered.

The Wingèd Words

What are these wingèd words
that have escaped the barrier
of your teeth?
      Nothing doing,
nor my fault the Ford
won't start and so
      as walked across
you become land,
        bedded be my wilderness
        bookish my landscape and sea
        a bridgeless head tease.
Would you deign me everyday
if nearly to you
I were to say : "hey,"
      would you find me
contemporary
if Aristide stood for options
betoken of banks on which
no pronominal carrier
can stand
or gaze upon singers sweetly singing? O Ramona . . .

my ocean is sold

my ships of steel

and all my nuclear submarines have drifted.

A man on the corner

begs experience

as moments pass   into the panhandler.

Were we the land's

before we were landed?   And then suddenly

things meant homelessness,

> *alas my youth disbanded*
>
> *asleep in the automatic*
>
> *teller machine booth*

while all the while

you stepped up to carpet

and a brand new skin product,

as sadly I am now comforted

by leather.   *brick upon brick . . .*

If Aristotle stood for options well

> *brick upon brick . . .*

a skin head with a leadpipe

in the conservatory,

> *brick upon broken*

neck, thanks to my skin

it only happens

in my shipwrecked sleep.

What are these wingèd words

that have escaped the barrier

of my teeth?

   Nothing doing,

an evasive act

as when the lights go up

and you no longer like

licking me and the thing

becomes thoughtlessness,

     lick upon lick

engineered, it's

autocratic eroticism, a person

to person phone call

to my personal she-history whip.

   Whose sovereignty?

   surrounded by working

   papers and men my markings

a downtown trench

circled by suburbs and upwards

of one hundred stories of sky.

It could even become our own arms race.

Ode on the Son

Your life like a wentletrap

awaiting clarity out by the sea,

not expected to go astray

with your beautiful or homely sister.

Your life like a curtained window

to wait by, stentorian smile

returning home from the ship,

the mill, the missile silo.

Your life like the essence of make

breaking apart, fine hair

pushes from your face

to carpet your beauty.

I am not made of this farce you claim

but the one who will finally finish

the spiral, how grand.

Then that man grabs you

by the hair in the five and dime:

and says: "don't try it."

Where is my field of wheat,

my flock, my ocean,

my arsenal, my knight errant.

Hush, hush, he is performing surgery

on your mother. Go down and tell fate

it will be a difficult birth.

Quiet your sister. The horizon

is spreading like spilt milk

and your father's gone mad with desire.

You must be the last stitch

left on his worn plan, answer now:

will you plow, row, gather onward my brother

or will you be father and welter.

Ten Still Petals

I dreamt
a petal's depth of hatred
            hovered at my ear
while vagaries worked
            to rough me up.
The flower kept
            darkening
            the more I lay passive
a gaseous mass in the manner
            of some spheres.

                    That night
                    was an escapade, the very last
                            impulsive dream.
                    I was so desperately trying
                            to shove you down,
                    the smallest floralized
                            egg cup
                                    burst.

One Moon
          orbits,
just high enough
          to threaten Peace
in a Vase
          or at least
transit's Beauty. Unbending

                    Dante waits
                    at the Gates of his beloved
                    Florence for his
                              Laurel cap,
                    while under glass
                              the specimens
                    who grow tired
                              of plight
                    are straightened out
                              by energetic wealth.

Deep Black takes
        precedence,
inside all falls
        but the undiscovered
touch of blindness,
        wherein My love
remains
        unbidden.

                Part of me
                thinks only of this. Your
                        half-shut lids fell
                sleepless
                        into my lap. A girl,
                I have seen tragedy
                        consider being
                such as we are.

Great lengths foregone
        to trap one leaf of
light. Valiant and yet
        the poems still spring
from corpse fires,
        the Isolated heart
        crawls up
to the cavity of ear
        and sleeps.

                Listen
                while dreaming,
                        Fear is circling within,
                the horizon is moving
                        secretly along
                your ever diminishing
                                home.

A memory anvil
        surrounds
the rose head. Present day
        cruel pleasure
momentarily dims
        true evil, distills
a more potent
            desire.

            Cyrus of split
                    parentage
            still ruled Persia,
                    despite aspersion or
            fatal trickery, our similar pressures
                    shall rise,
            controlled likewise in
                            silence.

I abandoned
        our mystical union
on authority of your voice,
        its mechanical
        chokedamp
enveloped my suffering
        until I was loath
        to give
the bicycle memory
        up.

        Coerced as such I came
            internally
        to blows, the plying will
            inside my head
        in turn did form
            a rim above the breach.
        I know there was a time
            when you alone
        controlled my faculties,
            but today that hour
        of abasement
            is finally come
                to an end.

Heinrich Heine lay
        lifelike
in his inhuman
        misery, his views
strove nightly
        to escape
the dying poet's body, knowing
        they'd flourish
beneath a healthier task-
                Master.

                These unfinished versions
                        hang like
                poisoned tendrils
                        disturbing
                the ignorance of the living
                        mystical rhetoric.
                In futures they may prevent
                        blindness and paralysis
                assuming the Mind
                        refuse détente.

Flakes of fire will dart
　　　forever
from the undetected
　　　counterfeit victory.
The lost moment
　　　of Hatred
lives on unfettered
　　　as a powerful show
of humiliation,
　　　ruining the dream
of further triumphs. In this way was

　　　　the Horror
　　　　　　of Harpagus
　　　　silenced by
　　　　　　self-loathing—
　　　　bred from the zeal with which
　　　　　　he'd feasted
　　　　unknowingly
　　　　　　on the abominable meal
　　　　of his kindred flesh.

Moving faces on the dark ceiling
       tell me
someone's coming
       through the window.
I lay unable to travel
       the carpet
fearing my fears
       in the telling
will dwindle to nothing
       but girlish
phantoms. An old record,

         Mozart's 40th
            transmits
         an important message:
            hold a road open
         to lift my mind
            away by hoof
         from these nightly
            hauntings
         feeling inside me
            as a thousand wishes
         left in the wake of
            arrested lives.

Driven to hellfire
          by latter day
Samaritans, Virgil
          puts his sandal
on the brittle grade
          of downward stones.

                    And so he enters the well-
                              wisher's field
                    of vision parceled
                              by Christian history,
                    shaking, yes
                              and yet still able
                    to cross off
                              evil innocence
                    and place the necessary
                              human misery
                    firmly back
                              in mortal question.

Underlying Assumptions

for George Oppen

The towering worry of fin de siècle

our spacious day,

      as all in an instant

flickering, we live uncalendared.

No wonder

your century cradled life compels

      one love after another.

We all fall in

seeking the archives of a careful choice—

      the hewn thin line

      of created memory,

dedication to thought & fellow

      across the crossing of moment

and moment's sense of latitude—but finding only

      your   long   life

as but a wink

      in edit's wedge.

Left to believe what leaves the mouth

will turn a profit,

we stand reading

      detect a rumor of bills and hear

         your voice

and recall

the pleasure of listening

the power of production

               "what we commoners have won"

this page,

and all its underlying assumptions,

and know again

there's place for us, and such

a country.

After First Figure

It is illusory

a fitter memory,

a prostrate signifier,

breach / bridge / causeway.

Knowledge lies   shrug

with capacity, got it, everyone

can give birth

and balance between pleasure wavering

(the impression kept) and

the pain of doubt.

This is a future, a coming

that is the ecstasy of non-abandonment.

The sad and fragile admittance

of taken space, is past imagined

pure linear advance

we grab on because we can,

because we are opposable.

Still the shunted

of course, of what is, is sheer sign.

And as with imagination

there is no choice

being thought bound

the separate mind stands out, as matter

and maintains dreamily:

"I have been over to the words and they work."

They are the future

rejecting the read (refinement)

as the attempt to sanity (processed)

"nay"

for no heeding choice is given,

as if the freedom to document

the seemingly dubious lighthouse light

could say more keenly: isolation.

Convenience must admit

exclusion in the rhetorical question

(a signal for logic)

We might lust for others, but never may

obscure meaning

in a claim of taken space.

Studio Life

So much for expansion!
The troops have withdrawn
to re-assess
the junkpile brotherhood
while we women are going
to look for a walk-up,
hot running water a must!
I don't know about you
but I'm certainly glad
for any percolator that comes along,
no matter what allegiance.
Say, isn't that Suave you smell of?
Come along, you can join us
if you lose that proclivity
for worship—any medium size
planet should do. Just think,
four walls and a microwave
could really keep us busy.

Club Life

The Goaders have gathered

for leaflet printing

and the ink is almost paste.

Hey Sarge, plow now, worry later,

then we can bring in those girls

from across town to spike the cider.

We can bromo-seltzer our enemies

into packaging this stuff,

our most valued asset—

nature walks galore.

This just in: Platform jumpers

have been spotted

spreading duty-free tablets

among the earth dwellers,

so send out for Folgers

and we'll pull those suckers in.

Jumping joysticks, spring

is causing a major disruption

in the hopeless sector—

considering its global persistence

it's a liability no patriot can afford!

Helena & the Regional Boys

Like recognizable streets

those Boys keep right on

coming down my heart.

I'm a gun runner

for the United Girls of Camp &

I want those boys

like a western crescendo.

I can feel it moving now

from the damp concrete

to a wet desert,

her and those jeans

all cued up for the punch.

I'll call her swaggerlee, or

the moment when the bar bathroom door

marries hook to eye &

shame gets a great big mirror all its own.

Into the Bedroom

Certainly deluded wisdom and all
those strewn packages from Christmas,
"scholar's disorder" keeps me covered
under this comforter thinking of us.
There there Erasmus, sinuous mind of love
in all its fibres off to Paris to see
what's become of an antique world.
Cut me a bolt of satin Vermeer
sing deep your told conviction,
lace up trussed up laughing feet
then turn your head and listen:
the parakeet doth chirp, the Moon
remarks my memory
and I am bending draped to brass
in pain and folly trembling.

The Removal of Enlightenment Safeguards

I

Entrapped   enwrapped
of one   in two

he drapes and bends
            filled with fingers

defying boundaries

II

The yellow air
of the room
surrounds
the place of vanishing
holes

III

The muscle but a case
on top
philosophy pulls
                he squirms
in the paradigm
flutters
with down

IV

Strength from behind
encircled
                man à clef
I grow phallic
with each dissemination

V

Soluble edge

     "the violation of sustenance"

continuing dribbles shift
bound assumption
the fence goes down
once entered by the weakness of protest

VI

Drooling humanism
          she boots him

VII

"Thou standing factory
          most vulnerable to exclusivity
risks a vicious strike"

Of hemmed-in vanity

VIII

The rope returns
a favor
cutting off circulation
and so by example
late for dinner

IX

The human body
prisoner of war without vestige

enlightenment evidence

During this Revolution
for Helena Bennett

Dear recondite shooter,

you're cupping me with dying, leaving me bloodless and loud.

Shoulderless Grace go back,

       and mean one garden of tallish grass

the waitless lucky summer with many a torso manned again

and handed Main Street this girl said: What about tonight?

It's you and me shorter one,

       with a bolder form of naiveté

then, for one tiny booted moment of largesse,

"her"

a vilified craving in night time,

       our sweet morning crib notes

and no familiar gene can not a Truth Tale Tell

it's only breakfast this life around.

I witness going back the many chewed things lost

your silence restive pardon of a sort I can't forgive.

Graceless I come query always

in hope of clearing this name from mud

finely how her measure could cover me like syrup,
a waffler I was, the edible beauty

will take this to her grave

but say something more endless,

than the strideress sleeps now with fishes

for it was us against the unbothered
and now my jet hangs mirrorless all
excuses for unbinding empty by her glances.

Ode to Protest

It's as if to be real

you and I must garner backers

without a rib to call our own.

We make ripples

with daily effort and then suddenly

flood the place with anger.

Ours is the anger

of the lowly,

we see life

from the knees up.

What vision we had

on that glorious day,

even the weather

stood aside and let us pass.

But because we could not write

our hearts could not be read,

and when we wrote

it's then we could not publish.

And so a so-called prince

came along and told our story.

He called us "feeble weavers"

ignorant fury

animal instinct

wild in the streets.

If only we had means

then we would give light

to meaning. But for now

it seems royalty will keep writing

the book on right-of-way

and we again shall lay

our lives by the wayside.

The Ballad of Her rePossession

wait,

and in the leap

privileged   peaceable   pursuit

    "for my God a . . .

mercenary faith

lays down with reliance   (nation)

convinced forthwith of   (science)

    "and into freedom I am brung . . .

<u>redemptioner</u>

cinched and touted believer

spouting audacious ideas of misery

    "for country and . . .

forsworn

to be in vision's peculiar benefit

complicit kin

or, stateside homeyness

SECONDLY

enough

ignorance

to fell unclouded truth, truth

like a tunnel to the heart

   fluttering

      "he put his hands upon me &

         I became equal in my lowlyness . . .

woeful

of what I knew, no mystery &

no splendor more splendid

than his sublime carriage, so

      "caress me in thine eyes . . .

gentle

wrong doer,

she spread for the promise

of blossoming

full   fragrant   fiduciary

& lied to

THIRDLY

waste,

in the mind waste

    "give my pleasure to the divine . . .

accuser

    "the pain of one answer . . .

under a God

in the long grass of summer

(wherein the stench of trash)

my mind (concrete)

grown big

in the eyes of the crowded state

idle   inward   individual

    "as I do not feel but know my love . . .

invisible

divisible

in despite

     "as I know I am woman, not man . . .

not manifest

FOURTHLY

I stepped off the prairie

no family,

the landscape does smite

God's country

    "could you but . . .

unravel borders (the village)

break from the broken promise (the city)

rescind distrust

    "for I came on shore . . .

<u>beholden</u>

hostage to the apple of my eye

    "and with these gifts I became . . .

learned betrayer & recreant

assuming my prerogative

precluded

by the bargain of heaven,

or, unimaginable products

FINALLY

the purchase

fled, before I could

flee,

    "all roads lead . . .

astray

whisper eclipse, sign of impotent witness

where angle may be read as love

the apogee of shame

    "he saved my life from . . .

saviours blind &

then with witless child

blinded me anew,

pronouncing:

bury your proud piety

I will no longer be

your gravel driveway

punished dreamer

failed redeemer

man, or country

Ode to the Man in the Mire of Babylon

after James Weldon Johnson

Because sometimes it's better

to be a dirty leper

than a beautiful Father

who would cut you soundly

should you rise above him.

Better to shun false respect

given freely to abject persons

of coldest intent

and remain true of heart,

though after the gold

has been meted out

you are left empty handed.

Where now is your quest for knowledge?

Ever since the happy few

distracted you from different pleasures

you've been craving your family

like a bitter remedy

and answering for needy sins

lending death the time it needs

to take true kin and run.

Choice cares not for the undone,

we live in the streets

because our fathers

are not beautiful,

they were turned out of the Temple

displaying too much vision,

their carts were without wares.

I am a cripple

for I inspire no envy

though your God may lay down

his back for my bridge

and I drag myself

to greener days,

we are still just exiles,

indentured to the ancient homeland

where we work not for purpose

but for fear of being locked out

with swine. What resemblance

have you to me except in all that's wanting,

for we alike can see that crevice

under the crown of pro patria

threatening to break apart

should we not come home.

Stay and enjoy the disruption

drink and destroy by loving hard,

do not marry or serve the unwanted master,

and fill your plate with forbidden oils,

toil no longer,

for when the cock crows and a new life is born

death has already won the battle.

When in Rome

No, I will not fondle you willingly centurial world
nor stroke your shred of decency, I hold no candles
or so you broadcast, ever since you kissed
my world weary decadence.
Hey soldier, go flaunt your swags and jabots elsewhere
this girl is bowing out, full to the glands with garlands
and Democrats, the truthful and bad will eventually see my way.
My webbing or weaving grows thick with all your travel plans
you tree trunk, you bile monger, you ghastly gewgaw
bereft of Metaphor, this time your ignorance will kill you
once and for all Centurion.
Didn't you notice your hundred years are up.

Cell #103
for Vladimir Mayakovsky & Fred Moxley

How many years locked up
does it take to create a Revolutionary?
How many a poet?

With our penal system
we shall give to you:

life, education,
punishment & hope,
hopelessness & tuberculosis,
a haircut & race hatred,
organized religion,
a personal God,
a place to sleep &
clothes to wear,
fear, slavery &
an alternate economy,
drug connections,
enemies,
allies & a new body,
romantic opportunity,
prepared food,
allotted time &
something to keep
for your memory's permanent damage.

The Right to Counsel

The mighty symbols
have snuck away
with human memory.
Actions are now
horrifically undressed
lest they should corner
the market.
One more docket
left silenced,
similar to the way
any words can fight
when given the story
of life and death.
In this quiet neighborhood
the people move around
like rabbits before dawn,
justice is untrusted
and visits no longer
than a speck
of dust or a trace
of conscious life.

The Right to Remain Silent

In foregoing witness
against ourselves,
what risk,
this clean towel,
or breakfast
intact by moments.
Fear the state
that could eat many lives
just hanging
on the hope of
divine punishment.
Singing together
we know not who
we serenade,
if not ourselves
who are no selves
and broken
we look to bedtime,
elope with big
distance in mind.
Space is a vicious map
erected by the
trampling of destiny.
If you can only live
one life, you must die
for those
you throw away.

Life Policy

Lit by the light
of one lamp,
with clarinet backdrop
& ashtray,
you pitch safety
and comfortable Futures.
Your neighborhood shows
as you trace the map,
ruffle the bills
and conjure up scarcity.
Everybody's doing it, you say,
Hopeful.
Take your big dreams, I say
through the back door,
no one here can sing fate
or pick up that dime, anymore.
We left crossroads back there
with compromise, one nation
two hundred miseries
and all that commotion.
Your dreams are just words
like table salt.
Me I know
this year's moment
will be 2 a.m., my life savings
and one train ticket
down the fault line.

The Nuptial Life

Given that coyness isn't working anymore

in store are various devices. Crises abound

as a lack of appetite consumes your gentry.

Your climber urge came zooming in and

ignored me. Perhaps you saw what tune

I dripped when the girls walked by.

Eye my sprawling furbelow then tell me

it's not effective—even bored henchmen

would find this outfit tempting

but low and beholden I'm left rolling

in my own digits, 100% silk.

The lilt of my filthy ways lie neglected

by these, your hand wash only constraints.

Reports poured in that lusciousness

was growing general, all over Providence.

I tried to go out with my hunger

but all that was left were types.

Kalypso Facto

The matrix of your hamstrung home-life

is undercutting all my generous gifts.

The current temper is such that soon

even the most bedlamite among us

will be threatened by marriage. Such

unalienable boundaries are bringing distrust

to all frolicers. Now the clouds show Zeus

is arriving to muck us up even further.

That hopped-up interventionist is thieving

all my island's hidden treason. His loud

armaments have been making petit fours

of continents for far too long. Now you

who once found me dainty are eloping

with Enyo. Your indiscretion may dress-up

progress in money lending but trembling

at the horizon I hear those othered lands.

We're all entangled in your strong-arm, but

fault me if we don't coalesce to curb

your second guessing with a dose

of our jilted memory.

Muse Couplings

History

My Clio, when will you let fall that ugly uniform
and allow my digits to stroke your dialectic?

Astronomy

Urania, the orbit of your rounded spheres
telescopes my eye on down your faded levis.

Tragedy

I saw you on a street corner Melpomene,
your big dark deals were courting the hopefuls down.

Comedy

Thalia, go call Melpomene into dinner,
he is trying to steal your girlfriend and call it fate.

Dance

Terpsichore, if you keep sporting those leotards
I'll be forced to fondle your castanets.

Epic Poetry

Calliope's muscles have upset my breastplate
his deep heroic flexing is well worth the wait.

Love Poetry

Erato the counterpane terrorist
has made me tipsy with his strong cocktails.

Songs to the Gods

Now that Polyhymnia has been put to sleep by Clio
I shall dream of his nipples having nursed me in fear.

Lyric Poetry

Euterpe, with the gorgeous chiseled face,
my sonnets only come in your embrace.

Neither Fish nor Foul

Your loopy tragedies have taken up just about enough
of this town's time, you surette, you maverick,
browsing around adulthood like you've shopped
here before, I'm sick of it. Your big confidence
invades my psyche with scattershot precision
and undermines all my carefully planned pretension,
but may I remind you I'm more grown up
than you'll ever be and I won't have your
fluttering lashes and flawless face
clawing up my already leveled kinship.
I'm going to kill your cash-built strut
and cut you boldly to the quick of your deep understanding,
I'll spill your ghastly evenings all over the Ivy League,
you know, those nights you've spent crying
by your claw-footed *baignoire*, praying your mother
can hear you from across town, or the upstairs guy
will see red circles under your eyes and shower you
with one of those seductions born and bred of sympathy.
The problem is your mother always comes running
and the guy always falls in love, I can't figure it out,
your lurid trick of appeals must be some bargain
because when I gain one speck of ground
you, like magic, become miss faux queen of the universe,
you walk in here and throw your lean wit
all over the badly framed Monet prints and
then prance off into every social circle from downtown up.
Seems you can knock down entire systems built upon
crushing us under, I'm under and you see it,
the perfect target for your sort, I'm here
like some loyal goldfish waiting for the flakes
to drop down on my head. But my thought can no longer
take your vagabondage, you faker, you false harbinger
of easy freedom, I'm kicking you off and cutting all my connections

as they embrace you one by one, you the unjudgeable,
you the "you don't know what she's been through,"
give me back my contentment and go crawl back up
whatever toxic riverbed had the misfortune to spawn you.

Dear J

it's not like I didn't know that you & joe . . .
I mean really, I know I'm backward but at least
credit me my century, after all, if we toss up
all those desire straws what's left but the pick-up lines
and a bunch of old Dylan tapes. I know this better
than you think, fainting couches and cozy domesticity
aside I've walked some low countries in my time
was once even brought near under by a heartless yodeler
in jeans & a t-shirt. If bad history doesn't get us
faded levis certainly will and crumpled love poems
in hand we'll all end up down the same dead end mews,
that Orphic landscape where every song sings
you are the dejected and I wrote this for you, damn it girl
cut off your hair, we'll make bow strings
and sail to the islands where we can write
shipwreck odes and have tupperware parties,
everyone will beg for our lascivious lyrics
and Sara Lee danishes, I'll bring along my Utopia
and you can bring your guitar if you promise me
you won't start a girl band.

Cast of Shadows

Niggling Spring, the distant palaver
of subjects in the craven bite
of the opening air, in wanders
a holster-wearing mussed Apollo
gushing the beckoning tirade,
bedazzled credo beloved of sports
and the yearly hoax begins.

In a moment good reason will be shunned
for the tinny whistle of the calliope,
the fragile petalled entreaty
of heart's-ease erase a tedious legacy
of schedule, shuffle the mind back
through a violent sequence of mise en scène:
mankind mismated to misery.

Cleaving still to it
humanity a coterie of cruelty
bends over backwards to forget
the sky's no nimble chariot
nor ever will be,
no matter the yearly rebirth
or self-induced labor we cop.

The brass light of day mocks
more readily possibility's hollow
following winter's shut-in drear,
gerrymandered love interests
come knocking down the heart block
demand a lamp granted, hope
and all across the sky, uninterrupted sun.

Duet #1 Wordsworth

Seal my fits with grey immortality,
and reaper slumber among the ruined
world ways, beauteous Lucy, much the yew
trees surprised us of the solitary
resolution of mutability.
Lonely she dwelt in independence too,
up my cottage strange passion leaps as few
men wandered by traveled Tintern Abbey.

Of two evening ballads I have written,
known intimations and reply: the ode
is a lyrical joy, a morning's march
among spirit lines. And did untrodden
expostulation miles above it cloud
composed mornings, the unknown April heart?

Duet #2   Keats

In my city Homer stood a muse dark,
a hand written lesson on after eve
vapors. O Nightingale, how many bards
have I? Endymion, whose face I read
when long stanzas stood nighted in a dream;
In the dark of pent Hyperion, where
keen looking fitful brothers did to sleep
fall down, and living poetry was drear.
Why this solitude, born of cottage fears,
written on the first of Chapman's disgust
to one vulgar December? O King Lear,
thou autumn after superstition gusts!

St. Agnes, I laugh the ode into me
once again, tiptoe on the sitting sea.

The Bad Choices Spy on Us Girls
after Frank Stanford

Tracy hit me in the head
with a mop frame,
the blood poured out like rain

She broke my mother's planter
and ran back down the street

My mother bound me up
when the sundown said "come out"
but the screen door wouldn't shut

Later on that very night
the street met at the circle
and split itself in two

We cut across the backyard
ignoring the dangers
of Mr. Kittridge

We wandered the canyon
in search of the forest

We found a tree fort
all gnarled and hollow

We spied older boys in the fort
with a Playboy, they threatened us

We ran for the pavement
where our feet got stung,
Tracy stepped on a stone

I went for the army
but the house was empty
so I grabbed my horse

Tracy couldn't find
the keys hid under the mat

We rode each other
around the palm
yelling "getty-up!"

We looked for rope to find a possum
dead beside the broken tools

He was filled with white worms like rice

I galloped out and jumped
a saw horse

Tracy pulled up
on the low-branch tree

When it rained we built
a home in the gutter
made of eucalyptus leaves

When the water ran high
we followed our brothers
to the floodgates
where they ditched us

We set up camp
under the pepper tree
Fred got a palm spike stuck in his leg

When I stepped on a nail
I limped to the wall
with a hole in my foot
and called off the war

Tracy took a shortcut
down the winding stairs

To the driveway
where Ted was run over
by his own car

He had survived three wars
and told us sugar on grapefruit
was against the law

Then Emerita danced to Creedence
in a carved belt

Billy broke his arm

Scott rode barefoot

Fred wrote Fuck You
on the neighbor's driveway in Eugenia berries

At night we turned very quiet

Through the doorways we listened

Our mothers cursed their mothers
when our dads left, they said

"We are never going back to El Paso"

Wake

In all such looks,

    I'm doubting

does it seem beside the day your passion asks an answer,

    below you lives a need

as the woe filagree of each life can with midnight's eye

    beg a listening ear,

    above you lives a want.

As if woven in,

    there are those,

    myself among them

who live a driven worry of the left

    behind, potential to deject a fragile mind

who build our lives in careful steps

yet,

still do leave the ruin of wondrous leaps

    and scatter chill around in keeps

like some powerful ancestral wall recalls a quiver.

Cope, if you can,

    I will walk you like a line

and in the frozen field of aim, beside the gift of all intention perhaps I'll cry away the day

perhaps I'll choose a different wreck

perhaps I'll live this appalling destiny

in the economy of night.

The Waver in the Orbit of Uranus Becomes
Unexplainable

I ask you, is it fitting to undo me by leaving
now that we know there is nothing out there
beyond what we can see?
I admit I've suffered from a "parallax of heart,"
born of a skewing jealousy and seen most evenings
in field-weary gazing upon your sleeping body.
From that angle all other worlds look bleak.
Though I will not call on heaven if you leave,
for I'm certain that the spirit is a one-eyed
pretender to the throne of painfree living
who has stolen all my daydreams for a shot at the beyond.

I suspect the water's edge is enamored of the water,
a quiver on the surface tells me not the wind
but the wish to drift will devastate the sand.
It is the future's focal infection, this insistence on death,
like when my mother and father cradled me
as the answer to each other's desperate tread towards union.
For this is a universe where things are not apparent
in their cruelty, but continual, and the sweetness of order
is increasingly evanescent. If I could hide this day forever
from the pleasure of renewal and banish all contingency
from happening I would, but I have never seen planet X
or the wooden ships on the Eastern horizon.
Up until now my life has faced West, sequestered
reason reaching for an injudicious kiss.

Ode on the Particle

Once time had a monopoly

on increments

and neighbors vanished

in minutes. No, it was not

due to the significance of concepts

but rather a case

of the bit

unnoticed. Once I waved

in totality

and lost everyone

on the planet.

In a silenced silent speck

passed by

all matter completely dropped out,

down fell

the sun, the moon,

the earth entire,

and could it speak up, no,

not without assistance.

This was no tribute

to the anxiety

of team players

but a rather sore history

of the arbitrary. I stood

limited in it

searching for existence

of the ideal finite body

and found nothing.

When finally

next to zero

I remembered motion

mass and all

I could not pass through,

formerly so many

formal tokens

now the essential links,

person to person to person

unmet. So forget

the time

you dwelt in insolence

pretending to be

unique, as you can see

the infinitesimal

has already scheduled

you in, as when

lessoned by life

you reach

to touch it.

Irrelevant maybe,

but ask a day

of those who gather moments

and discover by severance

the unseen connection

of any specific body.

Three Graces

ANTHONY

a peonie unfolds
through gentle balance,
what allowances he makes
in light of that wiry frame
are caught in a simple tilt
of head, a barely audible slur.
He shall certainly gather poignancy
from many beautiful women
by offering home cooked meals.

PAUL

is a rose and sleeps in history's
gateway, he wanders not lonely
but alone and cannot lay down
with reason, every season shall
accost his translucence while interiors
weaken his tenuous being. Will
he finally be treasonous
on his border walk or will his face
elude the chroniclers? Such
unknowns propel his pose of wonder.

STEVE

a bird of paradise stands stiff
beneath convictions bathed in
the erotica of energy. Yet
if still when in the company of memory
he crumbles and by the tisk of time
all random things do story his decisions
he of all remains the one. I do not understand
his impressive connections considering
all that vision. He is jeans
and a swagger, a cigarette
on which to bank one's future.

Today my mind became an elegy . . .

Today my mind became an elegy
to the chemistry of 4 dead chambers;
take those familiar streets away from me
or just leave me alone. While you chafers
came so slowly on my pillow did lie
a rash of tomb-like stillness just alive,
ceaselessly caught in bad eternity.

When my battered and dead chambers revive
poets will be chemists in rescue
they will then begin a strict enforcement
of sweet nothings and chest x-rays of you
who pledge unique affection, the climate
will break black and the earth offer solace
to elegaic minds who've lost their place.

Lucky So and So
for Elizabeth Willis

Ebbing in these lights of space
each tended for balance, pleasure
and for my liege, a niche,
we have built what we imagine
others building. Behind other
summer-lit windows
there must be wall paper
worth waking up to, but here
in the city of Multiple Backdrops
beliefs are shaky and quips
fly all the way Home.

And so I journeyed. My soulless soul
a darkened station full with notices:
"Psychic phenomenon sweeps the Nation,"
amazing what borders can do these days.
But I had a better outlook on life
when you walked into the room
looking like a winsome Nora Charles,
eyes full with gifts. It can be expected
I will be the whispers you inspire,
tucked waist & golden colored bracelet.

As a gad fly may I borrow evenings
from your Great Heart? Are you
still waiting for a kitchen-sill visit
from the little bird of careless life
or may I finish your daily rounds?
With no more devastation than fits
it seems the world is calling you up,
Miss Full-with-Novels, Miss Too-Many-Movies
taking pleasure like a secret cigarette
in a land where what we most fear
appears each night at 6 o'clock.

But behold it was a dream. It was
the year the phones went dead
on Mother's Day, though most mothers
preferred fully realized human potential
to letters home or regular calls. Famous
Women moved like landfill and marsh land
revealing structural flaws and saving
the wildlife. Lucy, Ricky, Fred & Ethel
were there too, but it wasn't a dream,
it was a birthday party and all the guests
were smoking Silk Cuts.

And now it looks as though my stove-top timing
really did make a difference. Though most
mornings I still get up bewildered. I've come
to believe impatience goes a long way
towards establishing duty and rabbits
scatter with only the slightest disturbance.
After all, assault rifles may be banned
but assault is still okay, though men
now ask politely whether or not
there will be food. With these convictions
we'll watch the sunset, if ever the skyline dims.

Kept from the circle of influence
you and I are spotting for brothers.
I'm falling in. Remember I'm an orphan
with a first-run movie of family memories
running a continual loop in my head.
From this moment on there'll be only
whoop de do dear, no more signification.
Communal gossip will keep me afloat
while you turn the city on your heels.
Immanence and transcendence will meet
at the Capital, everyone will be moved.

News stories had a particularly abstract angle
that night. All fortunes read:
"What have you done with your life?"
Tell them you have walked over thirty-three vistas
of dangerous westerns. I'll fashion Holidays,
100 ripostes and all the vestiges of glory
we need. You see, I'm not so envious,
it's only spring and you are only reason enough
to give up all requirements.

Though Crowded

I am not thinking of you
always, in separation our time
is queer requirement, the
impossible revelation
of a moment alone, or the
pale counting of debts.
Alone in thought my mind
now falters, accomplishments
are my heavy buildings reached,
they mark the jeopardy
of savings, must I think
of everything as saved,
the daylight, all the world
of time I want you in shall
pass ungathered. Will you
insist for love my life
must make effective changes,
while throughout this
makeshift home the rooms
are filled with savings,
photographs and books
acquired as if my very life
on them depended.
Tonight I saw the moon
in the faint sky of Providence
and I was moved no deeper
for the distance. You must
know what you've done
to my ambition.

Once Over

As of now
the tendency
is holding,
my leeway has come
unzipped. I know
there have been nights
when you have awakened
far too feathery for sleep,
fearful of stopping
and wondered
if I slept
in sound,
I'll say I've dreamt,
but my pieces
are not fitting
or generous—
You were causal today,
as always, but I won't
bow to wishing
or ensnare
my longing
in the backward beauty
of an unlived heroism,
or did you say hedonism?
You said "call me,"
knowing my voice
is slender by your
condescension. I have been
layered into something
unlovely, as if born
to live out the grope.
And you, you have been

gently bending over
the hopeless beam
of my unsightly tendency
to love you.

Line of Descent

By evening appearance
       ghostly gentle,
the universe funneled down upon
       your accidental hands
and I danced on wing tips.

This is a story lacking flight plans
or verity, remember
I was as hopeful as quoted Whitman.

By night's fall
       scenarios dreamy,
the attempted rehearsals of distance,
       perchance to exit
in various possible outcomes.

It was a long time ago believe me,
Persephone remained with her mother
in those days,
plotted against the lover's
       potential to love,
for even in a dreary life
       plans turn up.

Ray of your return, an apparition,

as out on the couch I

wept, derivatively.

In my storage you will father

        undue memory,

Yours, etc . . . I will watch no daily gestures

        but fondle trinkets,

this one stands for pocketed lineage,

Hemingway in the house, or

Ibsen's pistol.

Ode to Grief

I've built this staircase

down

to losing you

and now the basement

is flooded

with sunlight.

Fancy that, love

bows deep

in the strangest places.

I feel so lost

without your warping net

to drag me through the nettles.

For ten years

unerring

you've stayed

beside me,

becoming

my most

beloved sorrow.

Now I know

I could read

every book

at Alexandria

and yet somehow

still want

for joy,

for you Grief,

tender isolator,

have bound me up

like a commuter

left to cast

my bliss behind me

far away

into the past. I'll say

I shall curse you

as long as I live

but I won't. I'll surrender.

For you are not splint

or gentle injection,

you're the redeemer

who has dreamt me

in the waiting place,

a slip-shod small arm

playing vigil to

my own life.

Ten Prolegomena to Heartbreak

The better parts
of my lover's work
are never quoted in reviews, god knows
truth serum for the asking and I quote:
        "kiddo, the world is our oyster bar"
now put another nick in the tin cup of life
and let us spill I will you well,
lay the pennies out on the track
lest this grandiose ball room affair
turn out to be drive-through dining

I confided in the opportunity to say "yes yes"
but what came out was a fracas, the Avant Garde lover
of hope, I am such an inept navigator
of woe betide, a miserable egomaniac,
        and you've been single minded which I like, especially
when everyone else is dueling, I love you
like the poem I wish I'd written
In Memory of My Feelings or
how I stayed true to my heart and broke it
broke it and stayed true

If I weren't so blue
I'd be an old world curled in your outstretched palm
one upmanship on the high seas of dramatic endings
or a big budget house in the country
        in our next appearance we will keep you apprised
with hourly updates, pay off the press
beforehand, but first we'll write
a left and friendless lyric poem
to warn you that we're coming

Lines like these
should be outlawed, loves like these
are newly imagined powers of nature, pshaw
I spotted you before any will to destruction
        erupted, laying a dour trail of exit lines
while secretly dying to run
we jumped ship and wept, it was our way
I the Lumpen lover
you a well-spring of second guessing
I recidivism unchecked

The world is aglow
with beautiful speed and poets slow down to a stop
I haven't got time for the word
right now, no matter its
        implications, last winter we drank so much
we fell in love and forgot all about unity
the city and you are the truest
of forms, trust and reliable disbelief
all rolled into one sad strawberry
my weekend and my last ditch

Skin has a memory they say
but you are a brain child, look at him go
so what if the sentries visit tonight
hold my hand and swing it
        ditch the visiting lecturer and put on
your fedora, we'll throw a big show for the border patrol
leftist coveys and jealous lovers,
for the following Monday we'll take on
new and more earnest positions, teardrop
teardrop, all out revolution

In the chaos of daylight
the buildings come shining
into the rented chamber of my over-heated heart,
where have the hooligans hid your awards
    in a trapped bird my love, in a dark
and lonely place, the car
ten years hence
in a hospital bed
this I shall perhaps recall,
soft and powdery scented skin, apricot I trust

The best parts of my lover
are in the poems, don't be fooled
he is always serious or
    in love, you must promise to remember
for this is no hoax, it's a total failure
I the she the leased forever
known to have dropped
the incalculable prince
the remainder of all remains

Atavism in a dress
she is strolling to meet
your criminal past, armed
with just the history to see it
    you've a bigger problem than first we thought, buster,
they haven't made that part in years,
on the bus she dreams of filmic meetings with big scores
and they'll all come out to meet her
when she comes, killing limelight and beautiful men,
and you were so unprepared

Diurnal death creates a disjunctive aesthetic
insert the joker here, you'll need a strong
divining rod to reveal all the skeletons
those two tow around, deal me in the reddest red
        life is unfailing and yesterday
horrendous, children play
in Tompkins Square Park now where are you going back to,
debt certainly, debt and a smallish house
surrounded by field a father and mother
and all of the gall of heartbreak

Wreath of a Similar Year

A circlet ring of light
        beneath our feet
a door, a possible path
        of very best will,
placed before us
        in infinite intervals.
Such facets of mind
        might sustain us
if luck runs over, or love
        provide the lost,
more bodily
        forms of warmth.

The inconsolable mind
        has created
abundant distress—
        the scarcity required
to bury a world
        of living evidence.
Abandoned so, in an idea
        of innermost anguish,
we have become accustomed
        to the unheard music,
the quiet accompaniment
        of water,
being disturbed within.

Thought intent
          upon contentment
may temper the guests of our greater being,
          unearth
the hourly questions
          burned down from youth
with energy and light. As in the wake
          of awakening
wrong attemts
          and wrongful death
will fall adjacent
          careful Hope.

          Hope,
how strangely of untold direction
          it sounds, blind as
the first letter on the first stone
          written down
as if a wreath to circle
          the last sound spoken
on some distant, though similar
                    Earth.

www.ingramcontent.com/pod-product-compliance
Lightning Source LLC
Chambersburg PA
CBHW022033090426
42741CB00007B/1046